GUITAR ENSEMBLE I

SCORE BOOK

Editors: Sandy Feldstein & Aaron Stang
Cover Design: Frank Milone & Ken Rhem

Copyright © 1994 Beam Me Up Music c/o CPP/Belwin, Inc.
15800 N.W. 48th Avenue, Miami, Florida 33014

Foreword

This book contains ten ensemble pieces, correlated to *Guitar Method 1* of *Belwin's 21st Century Guitar Library*. All ensembles are written with three guitar parts and optional piano, bass and percussion parts. The recording is designed so all parts can be heard, or the guitar parts can be removed.

Guitar Method 1 introduces rests on page 43. To play ensemble music it is necessary to understand rests from the beginning.

Rests

A rest is a period of silence. Each type of note has a corresponding rest:

Whole Rest: ▬ = o = 4 beats   **Half Rest:** ▬ = ♩ = 2 beats

Quarter Rest: ≀ = ♩ = 1 beat   **Eighth Rest:** ❼ = ♪ = 1/2 beat

When playing a note followed by a rest you should stop that note from ringing. To stop a fretted note from ringing, release the finger pressure on that note. To stop an open string from ringing, you can either gently touch the string with your left hand, or use the palm of your right hand to deaden the note.

- CONTENTS -

**CD and CASSETTE
PROGRAM LOG**

Love Somebody

Folk rock tempo ♩ = 104

Use after page 10 of *Belwin's 21st Century Guitar Method 1.*

The Trolley Song

Use after page 10 of *Belwin's 21st Century Guitar Method 1*.

When The Saints Go Marching In

Use after page 15 of *Belwin's 21st Century Guitar Method 1*.

Teacher Suggestions:

The Saints should have a bright Dixieland style feel. If you have an advanced student, one who is comfortable with barre chords, have him/her play a rhythm guitar part using the following barre chord voicings.

Each quarter-note strum should be played short with an accent on "2" and "4."

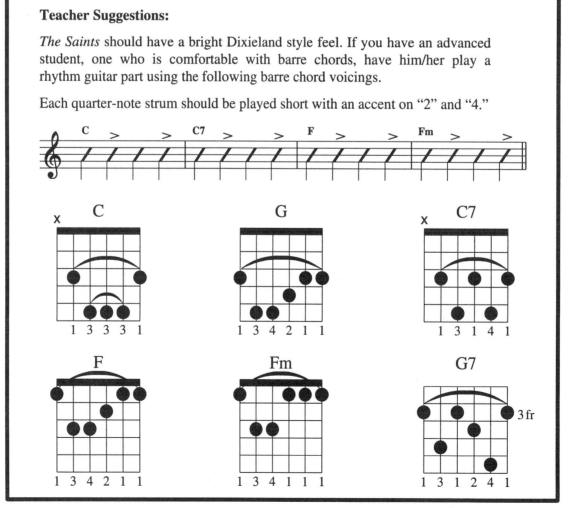

Down In The Valley

With a light jazz feel ♩ = 144

Use after page 20 of *Belwin's 21st Century Guitar Method 1*.

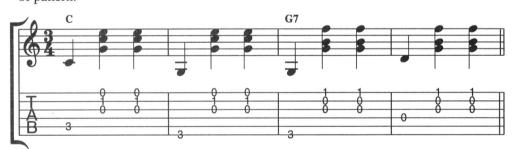

Teacher Suggestions:

To add a more authentic flavor try having one of the students play a country-waltz type accompaniment. The accompaniment pattern would be: bass-chord-chord. Since this is a two-chord song it's perfect for learning this type of pattern.

A few country licks would spice things up. Lick A works over the transition from the C to G7 chord and Lick B for the return from G to C.

Use after page 22 of *Belwin's 21st Century Guitar Method 1*.

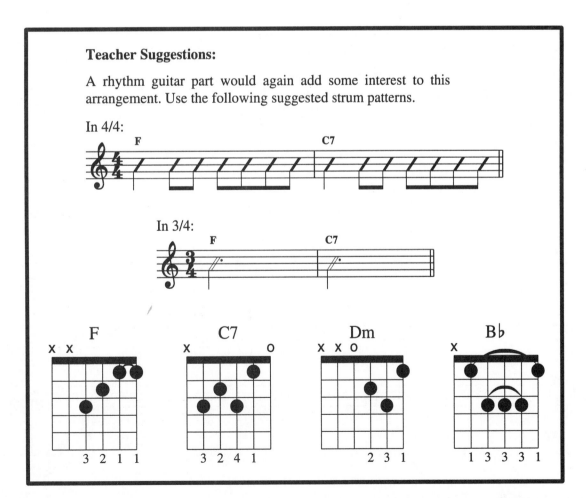

Teacher Suggestions:

A rhythm guitar part would again add some interest to this arrangement. Use the following suggested strum patterns.

In 4/4:

In 3/4:

Dona Nobis Pacem

Use after page 25 of *Belwin's 21st Century Guitar Method 1.*

28

Use after page 30/33 of *Belwin's 21st Century Guitar Method 1*.

Teacher Suggestions:

All of the notes and chords contained in *Blue Rock* are learned in the student book by page 30. The eighth note strum patterns included in the third guitar part are taught on page 33. You can begin to play this song after page 30, adding Guitar 3 after page 33.

Minuet

J.S. Bach
Arr. S. Feldstein

Use after page 36 of *Belwin's 21st Century Guitar Method 1*.

Blue Moon

Lorenz Hart
Richard Rodgers

Use after page 40 of *Belwin's 21st Century Guitar Method 1*.

Goin' Home Boogie Blues

Use after page 45 of *Belwin's 21st Century Guitar Method 1*.

Goin' Home Boogie Blues is a blues in "A." Since the key signature of A has not been introduced yet, the song is written without a key signature.